Easter Time Is Here!

HE IS risen

I0098729

Celebrate!

Judy Luca

Easter time
is here

A very special
time of year

A time to celebrate the love
in you and me

A time that gives us all
hope and sets our soul free

A very long, long
time ago

A great teacher lived
to help us grow

He taught us that
we are all one

And that he was
God's precious son

Jesus is his name

For all of us he came

To teach us
unconditional love

And to Shine Divine
Light from above

Jesus walked peacefully
upon the land

Teaching us how to live
as best we can

His lessons of love
were always at hand

Even though many did
not understand

He loved everyone
anyway

And prayed they would
understand some day

Jesus taught others
to see the Light

To help him spread a
vision so bright

He wanted everyone
to know

How in Faith and
Love to grow

He wanted everyone
to see

The greatness that
we each could be

He healed the sick and
helped blind men see

He brought miracles
for you and for me

He did his best to
show the way of peace

So the negativity of
the world would cease

He wanted all people
to live in joy

Every single girl,
every single boy

His time on the earth
wasn't very long but

his message of love to
this day lives on

Love
Remains

Even though his last
days of life were bleak

It has a special name
we call it Holy Week

HOLY WEEK

Jesus knew his life was
coming to an end

So he spent it being
together with his friends

He washed their feet
to show his gratitude

with tenderness his
love he renewed

He knew his disciples
would carry a very
heavy load

As they brought his
teachings on the long
and dangerous road

love

They had a special meal
we call it the Last
Supper

It was his last meal
before he had to suffer

They shared wine and
bread at their reunion

today we remember by
sharing communion

Jesus was punished by
people who feared him

He died on the cross asking
God to forgive them

After 3 days Jesus rose
from his grave

And his Spirit lives on
reminding us to be brave

Christ is Risen

rejoice
IN
hope

At Easter we rejoice that
Jesus' spirit lives on

In the love in our hearts
from sun up to sundown

Happy Easter

REJOICE AND BE GLAD

Dedication

This book is dedicated
to the Brilliant Light and
Unconditional Love that is
Jesus

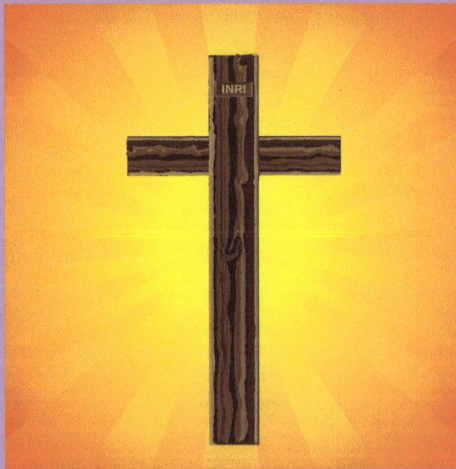

If you like This Book Take a look at my other Books

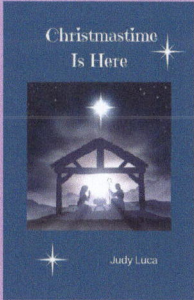

Christmastime Is Here

Christmastime Is Here" is a colorful, creative book to introduce children to Jesus. A tender, sweet, spiritual introduction to the glorious gifts of love, light, peace, joy and unity that the teachings of Jesus show us all.

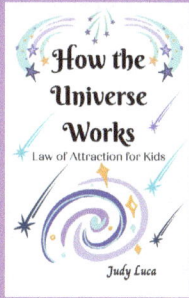

How the Universe Works — Law of Attraction for Kids

"How the Universe Works" is an introduction to the Laws of Attraction and Vibration for kids from ages 6-9.

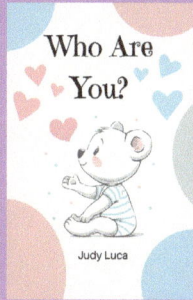

Who Are You?

"Who Are You?" is a delightful children's book devoted to letting the precious little ones in your life know how special they truly are. "You are Light, you are Love. You're a miracle from above." An inspirational book that is perfect for bedtime or anytime!

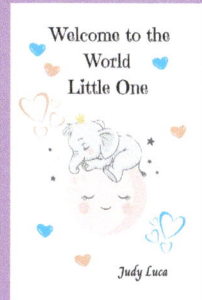

Welcome to the World Little One

When my first child was born the first words I ushered to the beautiful miracle in front of me was "Welcome to the world little one". I was filled with love, awe and wonder as I welcomed my baby girl into my life. Sit back, relax and read this book as you welcome the precious little ones in your life into the world.

Good Morning World

Judy Luca

Goodnight World

Judy Luca

The Song in You

Judy Luca

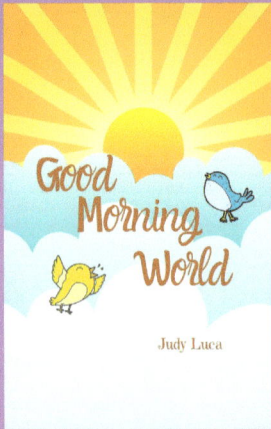

Good Morning World is a beautiful picture book to brighten up any day with your children. A perfect way to begin each new day with any toddler, pre-school or kindergarten child. "There's magic in the morning as the sun kisses the earth."

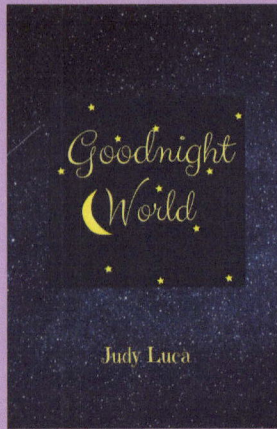

Goodnight World is a colorful bedtime story to help little ones so "...so their dreams will be sweet and their morning will be bright."

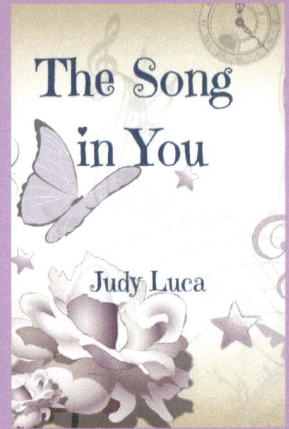

Every child is a glorious gift to the world. "The Song in You" is dedicated to the brilliant expression of life they truly are.

Kisses

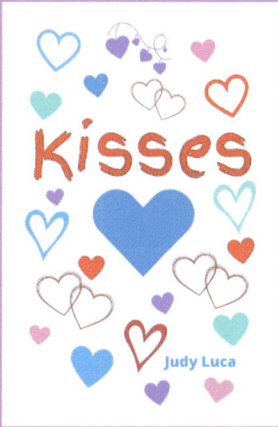

Kisses is a colorful picture book for toddlers to kindergarten children. They will delight in the adorable pictures as you shower them with kisses. A perfect bedtime or anytime story to share with the little ones in your life as " I kiss you once and kiss you twice, kissing you is so very nice"

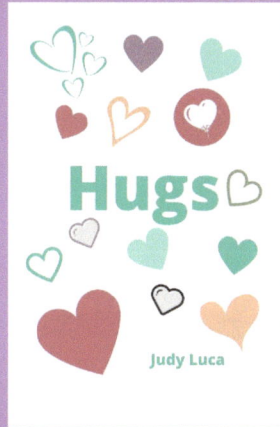

Hugs

Hugs is a beautiful picture. Dedicated to my dad who gave the best hugs. Your child will love the illustrations and the love your hugs will bring them each day! Perfect for bedtime or anytime. Cuddle with the little ones in your life and share some hugs!

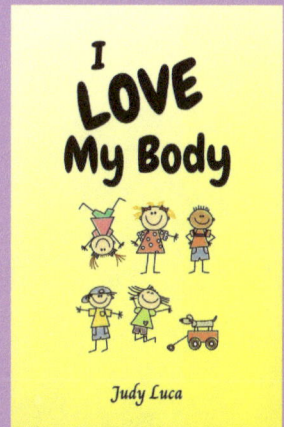

I Love My Body

Love My Body" is a colorful book for baby and preschool children to learn body parts and develop a positive and healthy body image! Brighten your child's life with this delightful book!

www.ingramcontent.com/pod-product-compliance
Lightning Source LLC
Chambersburg PA
CBHW041800040426
42447CB00005B/273